How Does it Work?

Contents

How do these things work?

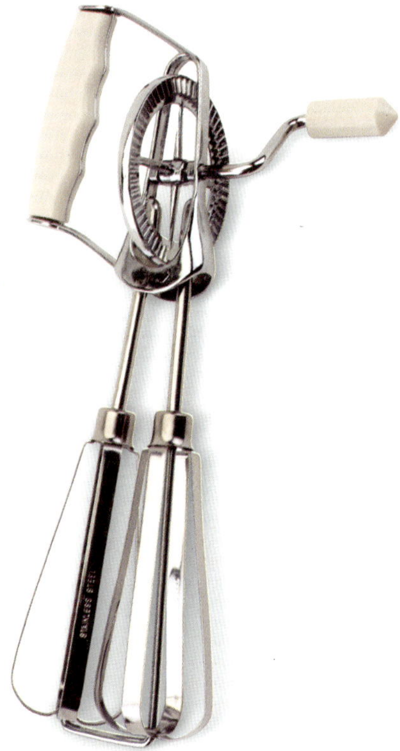

UNIVERSAL

Whisk

How does it work?

The handle is turned.
The whisks go round.

Water wheel

How does it work?

The water pushes the paddles.

The wheel goes round.

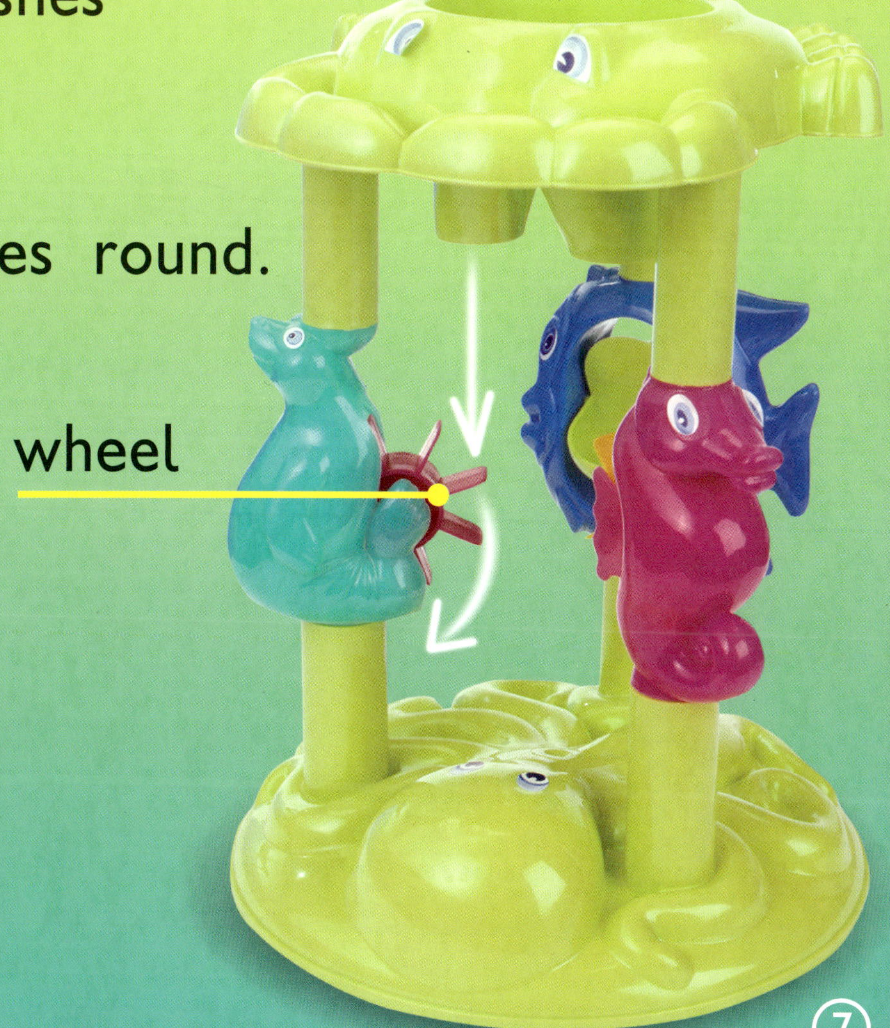

Pizza cutter

How does it work?

The handle is pushed.

The wheel goes round.

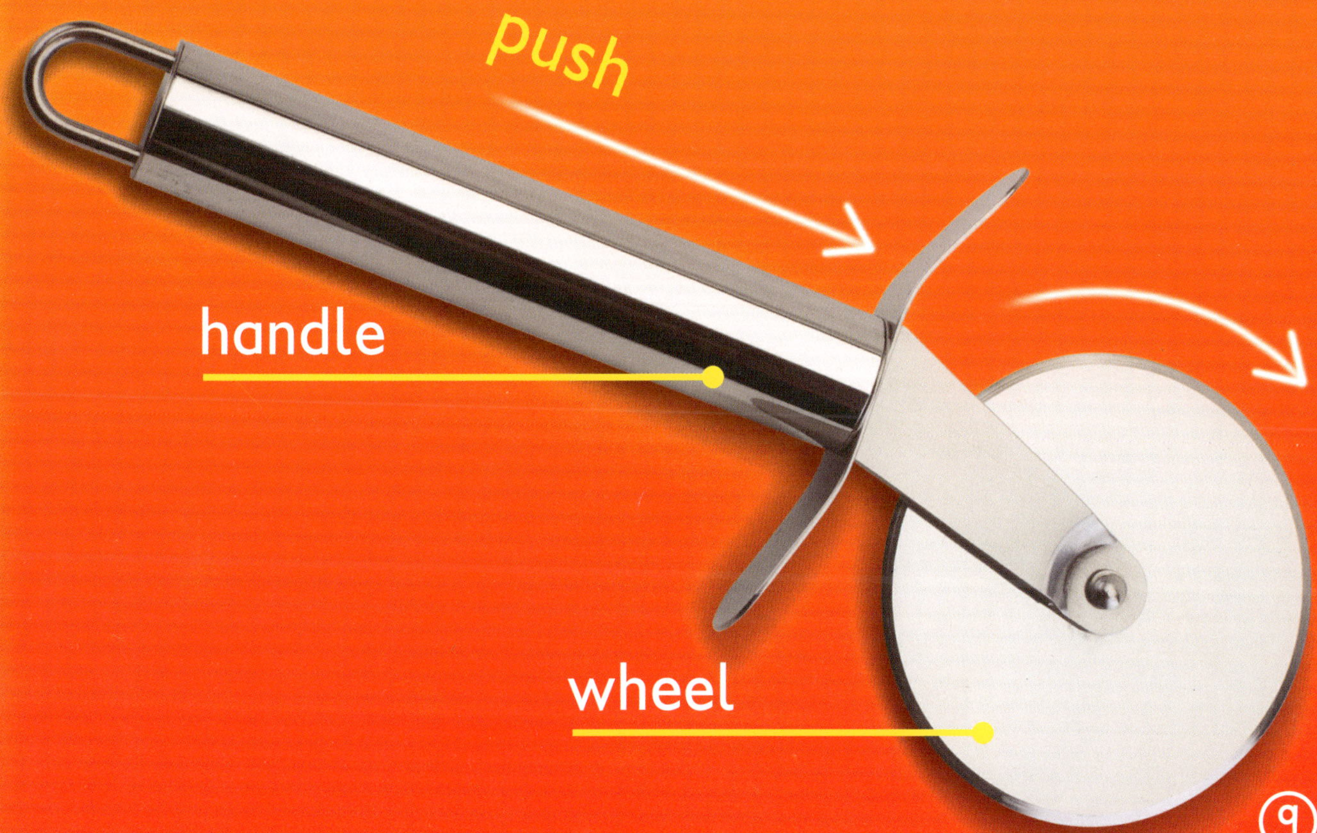

Bicycle

How does it work?

The pedals are pushed.

The wheels go round.

Toy

How does it work?

The string is pulled.
The wheels go round.

Windmill

How does it work?

The wind pushes the sails.

The sails go round.

How do these things work?

paint roller

car

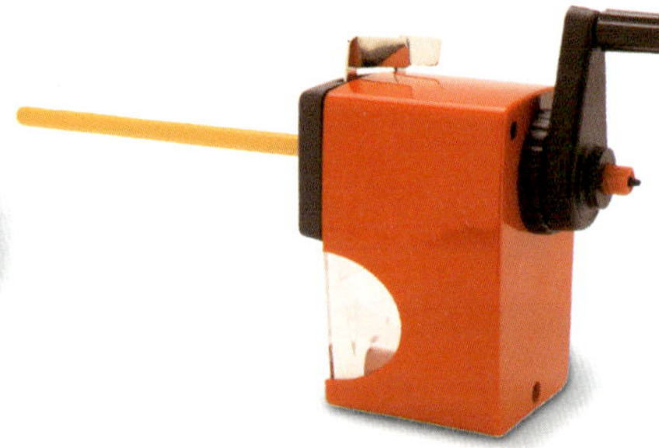

pencil sharpener

spinning top

windmill

wheelbarrow

or

Learn phonics with

Actipho[illegible]

Lorna S[illegible]rt

Written by Greg Cook

Phonics consultant: Kate Ruttle
Physical literacy consultants: Dr. Lowri Cerys Edwards and Dr. Lucy Jane Griffiths

LADYBIRD BOOKS

UK | USA | Canada | Ireland | Australia
India | New Zealand | South Africa

Ladybird Books is part of the Penguin Random House group of companies whose addresses can be found at global.penguinrandomhouse.com.
www.penguin.co.uk www.puffin.co.uk www.ladybird.co.uk

Penguin Random House UK

First published 2021
001

Printed in China

A CIP catalogue record for this book is available from the British Library

ISBN: 978-0-241-39063-4

All correspondence to:
Ladybird Books
Penguin Random House Children's
One Embassy Gardens, 8 Viaduct Gardens, London SW11 7BW

Tips for grown-ups

Actiphons is an energetic phonics programme designed for young learners.

Each of the 70 collectable stories stars its own playful character and practises their letter sound and action. By reading the stories in order, children will build their phonics skills and become active, lifelong readers.

How to help your child to read

- Read the words in small type and encourage your child to read the words in big type. Remind them to sound out and then blend together the sounds in each word to read it. For example, "**j-o-g**, jog", "**s-ai-l**, sail" or "**qu-i-ck-er**, quicker".
- If your child struggles with a word, help them to sound it out. If they still find it difficult, just read the word to them and move on.
- You can use the activities at the back of this book for extra practice. Have fun!

Lorna Sport loves to stretch and jump.

Sport is such fun.

Cool shorts, Lorna!

Lorna likes playing football.

Lorna also loves to play cricket.

You need a bat
for this sport.

And sometimes, she goes for a morning swim.

She can do amazing tricks on the trampoline, too!

Lorna enjoys every sport.

But most of all, Lorna likes helping her friends.

She cheers them on and helps them to do their best.

She uses her stopwatch to time the others.

Lorna uses her whistle to start races.

Then, Lorna's friends have a good idea.

They ask her to organize Sports Day!

Lorna organizes a great Sports Day.

Lorna gets a special medal for being a good coach!

Your turn!

or

Can you touch your toes like Lorna Sport?

Sit on the floor with your legs straight.
Reach forward and try to touch your toes!

To see a video of this action, listen to the story or sing the song, go to **www.ladybirdeducation.co.uk**. Click **'Unlock book'** and enter this code:

p6uUCGXegf

What next?

Talk about it

- Can you remember some of the different sports that Lorna Sport likes?
- Do you think Lorna deserved her medal at the end of the story?

Phonics fun

- Can your child find the **or** sound in Lorna's name? Emphasize the sound as you say the name.
- Give your child the storybook, and challenge them to find and read five words containing **or** as quickly as they can.

Get active!

- Ask your child to practise doing Lorna's signature move, sitting on the floor with legs straight, and trying to touch their toes. Can they reach? Ask them to make Lorna's **or** sound, or say a word that contains that sound, every time they reach slowly forward to touch their toes.

Turn the page to find your next Actiphons story!

Collect Actiphons Level 2